yukismart.com/

body

corpo

head

testa

face

faccia

grow up

crescere

back

schiena

chest

petto

bottom

sedere

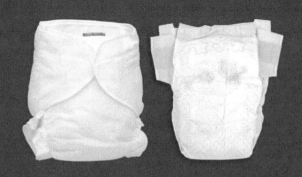

diaper

pannolino

eye

occhio

glasses

occhiali

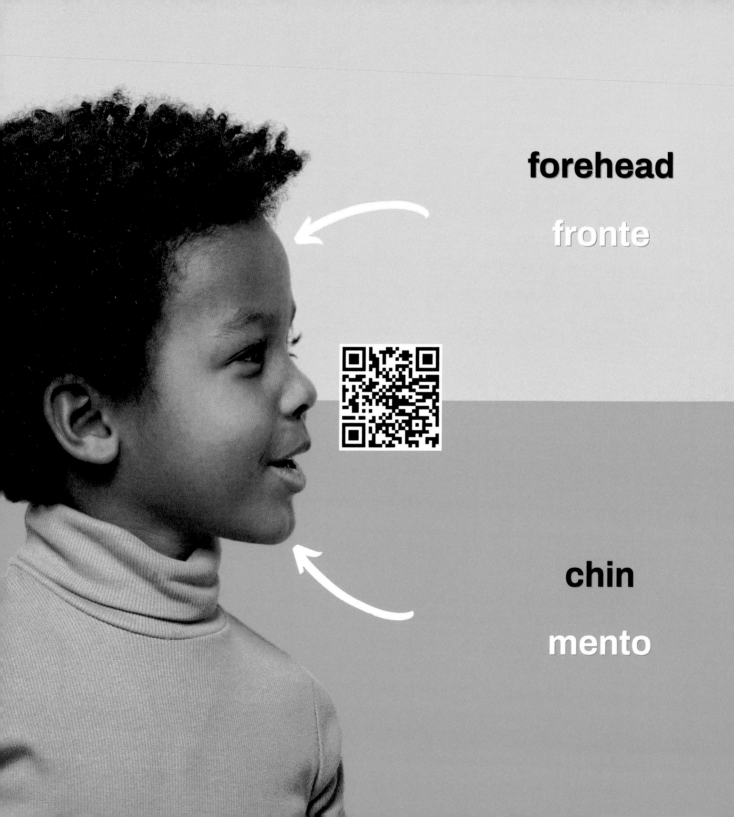

forehead

fronte

chin

mento

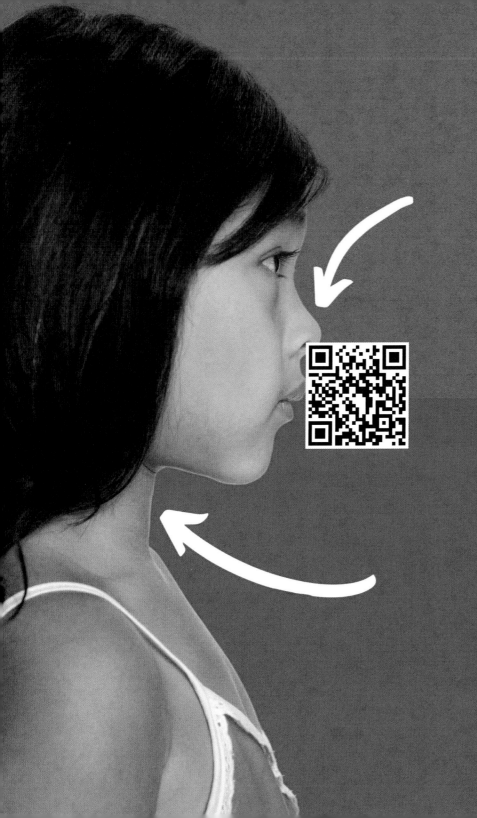

nose

naso

neck

collo

ear

orecchio

cheeks

guance

kiss

baciare

mouth

bocca

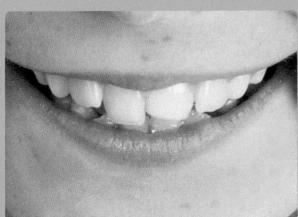

teeth

denti

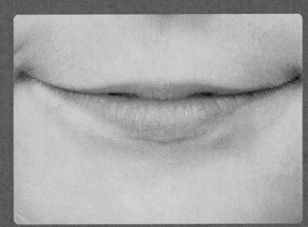

lips

labbra

tongue

lingua

hair

capelli

straight hair

capelli lisci

curly hair

capelli ricci

black hair

capelli neri

brown hair

capelli castani

ginger hair

capelli rossi

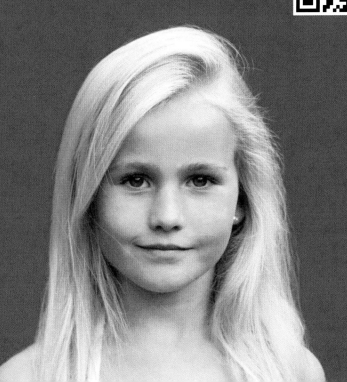

blond hair

capelli biondi

gray hair

capelli grigi

bald head

testa calva

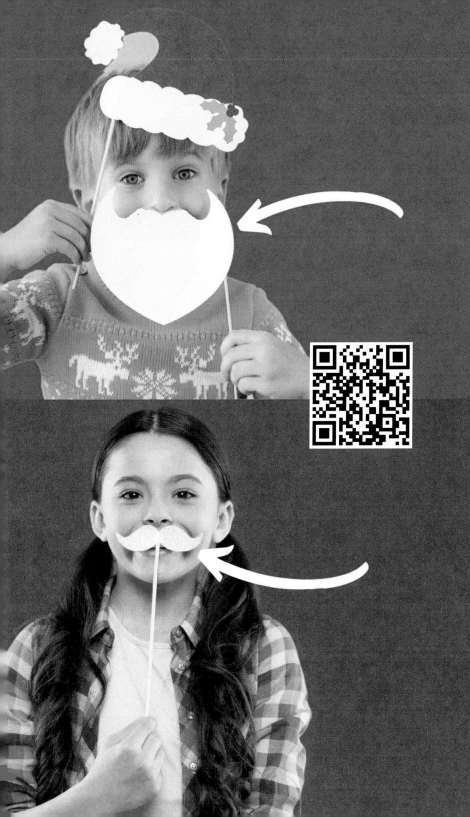

beard

barba

moustache

baffi

arm

braccio

elbow

gomito

hand

mano

fingers

dita

thumb

pollice

belly

pancia

navel

ombelico

foot

piede

leg

gamba

heel

tallone

thigh

coscia

ankle

caviglia

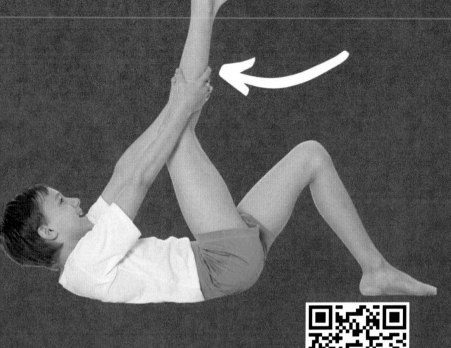

calf

polpaccio

nails

unghie

knee

ginocchio

necklace

collana

bracelet

bracciale

hat

cappello

scarf

sciarpa

coat

cappotto

pullover

maglione

pants

pantaloni

dress

vestito

rain boots

stivali in gomma

socks

calzini

shoes

scarpe

mittens

muffole

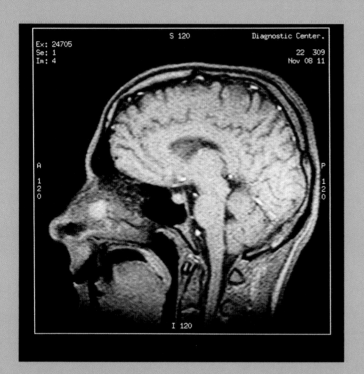

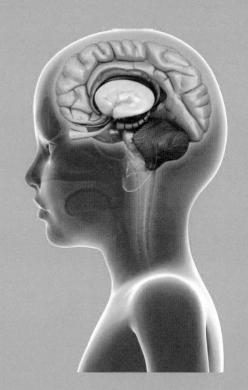

brain

cervello

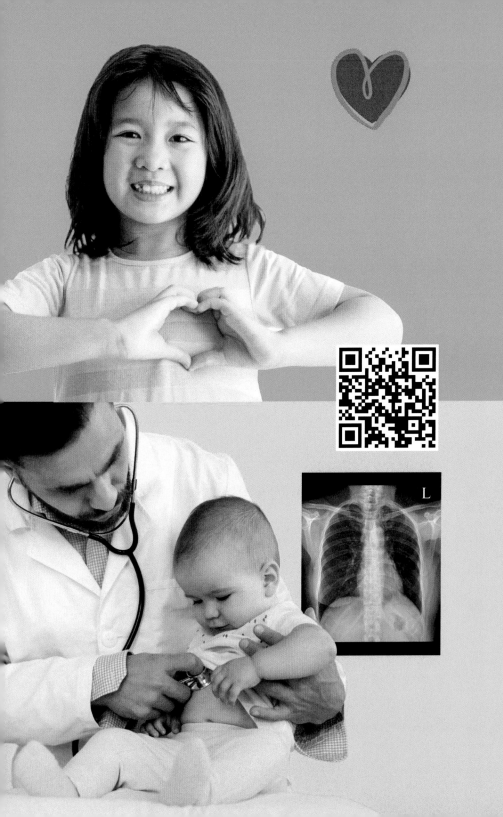

heart

cuore

lungs

polmoni

skin

pelle

sunscreen

crema solare

sun glasses

occhiali da sole

soap

sapone

toothpaste

dentifricio

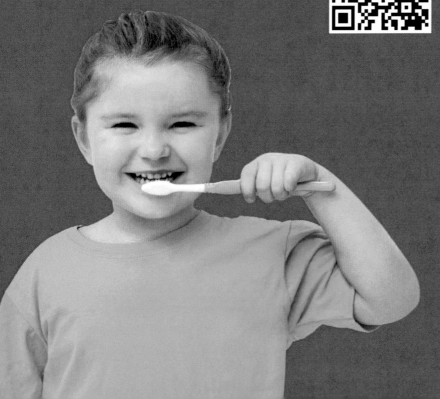

toothbrush

spazzolino

pain

dolore

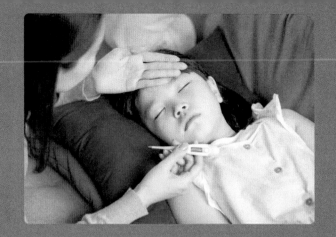

fever

febbre

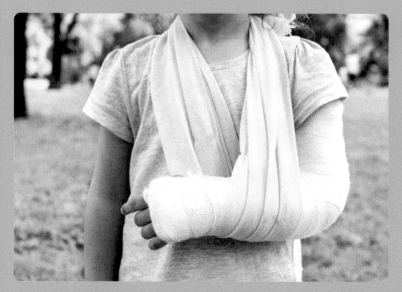

broken arm

braccio rotto

sneeze

starnuto

cough

tosse

dental cavity

cavità dentale

pharmacist

farmacista

medicine

medicina

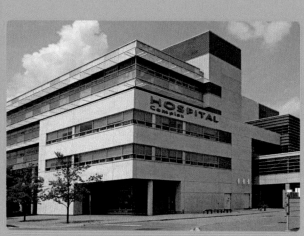

hospital

ospedale

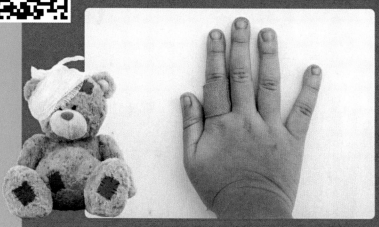

bandage

benda

paramedic

paramedico

firefighter

pompiere

firetruck

camion dei pompieri

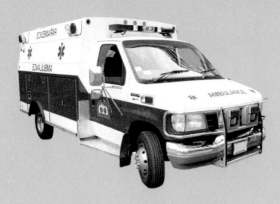

ambulance

ambulanza

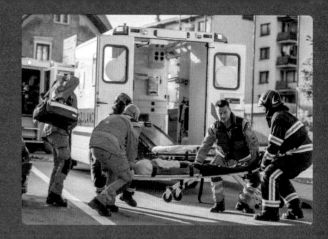

rescue team

squadra di soccorso

helicopter

elicottero

boat

barca

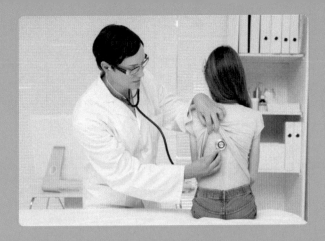

doctor

dottore

nurse

infermiere

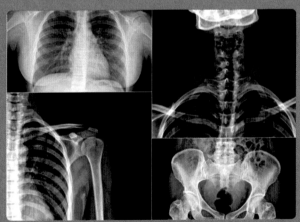

x-ray

raggi x

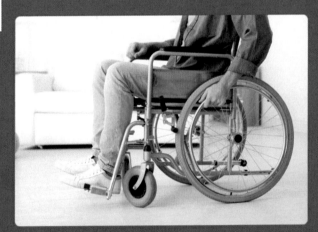

wheelchair

sedia a rotelle

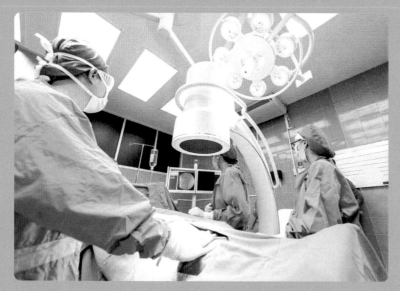

surgeon

chirurgo

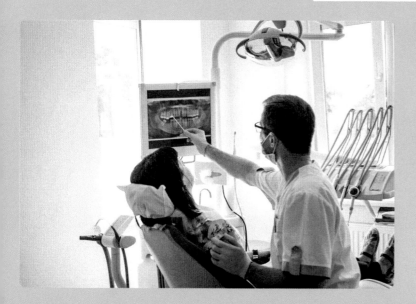

dentist

dentista

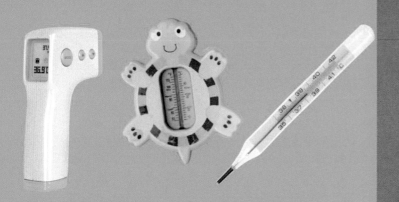

thermometer

termometro

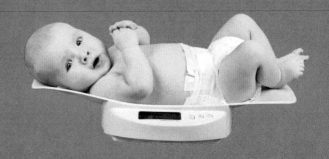

scale

bilancia

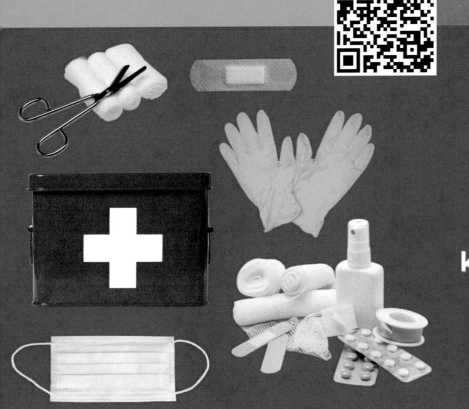

first aid kit

kit di primo soccorso

vet

veterinario

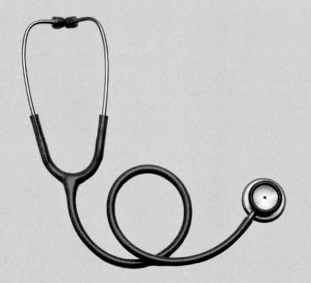

stethoscope

stetoscopio

dancing

danza

basketball

pallacanestro

soccer

calcio

swimming

nuoto

skiing

sci

judo

judo

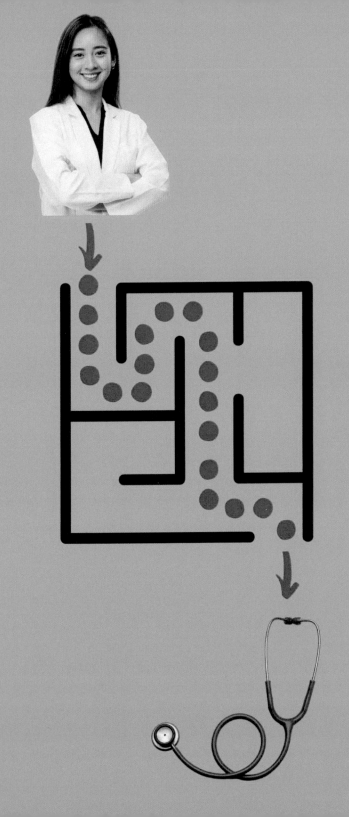

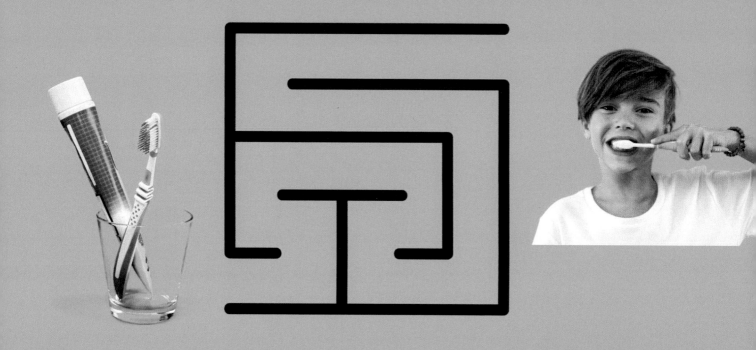

Made in the USA
Las Vegas, NV
15 August 2024